VICTORIAN
HOUSEBUILDING

Kit Wedd

SHIRE PUBLICATIONS

Published in Great Britain in 2012 by Shire Publications
Ltd, Midland House, West Way, Botley, Oxford OX2 0PH,
United Kingdom.

44-02 23rd Street, Suite 219, Long Island City, NY 11101,
USA.

E-mail: shire@shirebooks.co.uk   www.shirebooks.co.uk

A CIP catalogue record for this book is available from the
British Library.

Shire Library no. 667.   ISBN-13: 978 0 74781 095 7

Kit Wedd has asserted her right under the Copyright,
Designs and Patents Act, 1988, to be identified as the
author of this book.

Designed by Ken Vail Graphic Design, Cambridge, UK
and typeset in Perpetua and Gill Sans.

Printed in China through Worldprint Ltd.

12 13 14 15 16   10 9 8 7 6 5 4 3 2 1

COVER IMAGE
Illustration from *Les métiers et leurs outils*, published in
1876. Although the busy building site depicted here is
in France, many of the tools and activities are the same
as those used at the same time in Britain and there is an
identical reliance on human muscle to power every aspect
of construction work.

TITLE PAGE IMAGE
A bricklayer's labourer with a loaded hod, from a
Punch cartoon; his master is raising the first floor of
the house. The Irish labourer is advising a more recent
immigrant that he should ditch his farming aspirations and
become a labourer too – he would get paid just to carry
bricks up a ladder, while the master does all the hard work
laying them!

CONTENTS PAGE IMAGE
A decorative panel with a mask and foliage below the
first-floor window of a house of about 1880 in Ealing,
West London. The undercut detail and fine lines of pure
lime putty in the joints show that this is carved brick,
rather than a ready-made, moulded terracotta panel.

ACKNOWLEDGEMENTS
Illustrations are acknowledged as follows:

Alamy, page 17; Patrick Baty/Papers and Paints, page 41
(bottom); Bristol Museums, Galleries & Archives, page 15;
British Library, page 4; British Museum, pages 12 and 48;
English Heritage, page 44; Geffrye Museum, page 39
(top); Rob Jennings, page 16; Local History Library,
Southwark Culture Services, pages 10 and 24;
Courtesy of Manchester Libraries, Information and
Archives, Manchester City Council, pages 26 and 27;
Mary Evans Picture Library, cover image; The Regency
Town House, Hove, page 37 (inset); Rescued by Rover,
pages 22–3; Russell Butcher, pages 14, 19 (left), 28
(both), and 30 (bottom); Victorian Images Collection/
R. Cosens, page 25.

All other images are from the author's collection. Thanks
to Treve Rosoman at English Heritage for access to
photograph the images shown on pages 7 (both), 18 (top
left), 29 (bottom), 38 (bottom right), 40 (right) and 54.

Shire Publications is supporting the Woodland Trust, the UK's leading woodland conservation charity, by funding the dedication of trees.

CONTENTS

INTRODUCTION   4

SUBURBAN DEVELOPMENT   10

HOUSE DESIGNS   16

ON SITE   21

WORKING LIFE   45

CONCLUSION   53

FURTHER READING   55

INDEX   56

INTRODUCTION

The fact is that the mid-Victorian builders of our city streets are, historically speaking, a lost tribe.

SIR JOHN SUMMERSON, describing the London building trade, stated a melancholy truth: while the achievements of eminent nineteenth-century architects and a few successful contractors are celebrated, the lives of the craftsmen, apprentices and labourers who built England's Victorian cities and suburbs have received little attention outside academic publications. We know comparatively little about daily life on the small-scale speculative building site.

This book explores the day-to-day life of the sub-contractors and craftsmen who built the residential suburbs that represent the bulk of the Victorian construction industry's output. Where did these men get work? How did they learn their trade? What did they wear? What were their wages and how did they spend them?

London Going Out of Town, or the march of bricks and mortar, 1829. George Cruikshank's cartoon vividly depicts the unstoppable spread of the nineteenth-century suburb.

LONDON going out of Town. — or — The March of Bricks & mortar.

The cheerful, cosy home of a carpenter's family in 1850. Papa's watch chain and seal, and the doll he has brought home, indicate steady employment in a time of prosperity. A loaded bookshelf suggests a commendable desire for self-improvement.

One detailed account of the Victorian builder's materials and methods occurs in the novel *The Ragged-trousered Philanthropists* by Robert Tressell (1870–1911), published posthumously in 1913, which was inspired by the author's experiences as a housepainter. His builders inhabit a world of sweated labour, cowed by bullying foremen and the constant fear of dismissal. Worse, forced to 'scamp' their work to increase the firm's profit, they are prevented from exercising true creativity or craftsmanship.

The relentless misery of their working lives is described with a righteous indignation that reflects Tressell's socialist principles. Less subjective but equally disturbing is the factual evidence amassed by Henry Mayhew (1812-87) in the 1840s and '50s and by Charles Booth (1840–1916), a generation later. Their detailed studies of London's poor revealed how labourers and even experienced craftsmen struggled on low pay, and could be made destitute by accident or illness.

Other sources present a more optimistic view of respectable artisans earning steady wages. Middle-class helplessness in the face of builders' dirt and disruption, and their uneasy sense of being overcharged for bodged work, are recurring motifs in the satirical magazine *Punch*, which habitually portrayed the British Workman as cheerful, somewhat devious, and sardonically witty.

To 'scamp' was to cut corners and skimp on materials – a long-established practice of speculative builders at the lower end of the housing market. It could have disastrous results, as in this *Punch* cartoon of 1876 depicting 'the way we build now'.

'Middle-class cottages', 1878, designed by Richard Norman Shaw to demonstrate a new patent cement slab: an example of a first-rank architect designing for modest, speculative housing. The innovative building system is disguised with traditional tile-hanging to give it a fashionable yet reassuringly familiar appearance.

The professional and trade press also provide insights into the Victorian builder's world. Journals such as *The Builder* (founded in 1842) and *Building News* (1855) introduced new products and techniques, explained building and town planning legislation, and – most influentially – published detailed house designs. What the specialist press illustrated one year, the suburban developer's men would build the next.

Books were another rich source of information for the Victorian builder. In 1834 J. C. Loudon (1783–1843) published his small-format, two-volume *Encyclopaedia of Cottage, Farm and Villa Architecture*. Describing house design and construction with plans, elevations and illustrations of every detail, it quickly became the Victorian architect's and builder's bible. The spread of literacy created a market for cheap technical manuals, served by a separate, specialised branch of the publishing industry. By the 1890s, pocket editions such as *The Art of Building*, one of dozens of titles in 'Weale's Scientific and Technical Series', could be bought for a couple of shillings.

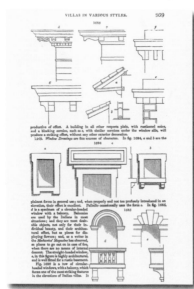

A page of 'Italian cornices' from Loudon's *Encyclopaedia*, with text wrapped around small illustrations in a new style of layout derived from the author's background as a magazine editor.

6

Left and below: Builders could order materials from illustrated builders' merchants' catalogues depicting every item needed to complete a new house, as seen here in a selection of door furniture in Pemberton's catalogue from the 1860s.

The most enduring evidence of builders' work is the mass-produced housing of the period. In the rural building tradition, house design reflected the site, local building materials, climate, and occupants' specific requirements. Construction was an evolving process: builders could adjust the design as they went along, and even a professional architect's drawings might be regarded as suggestions to be modified as required.

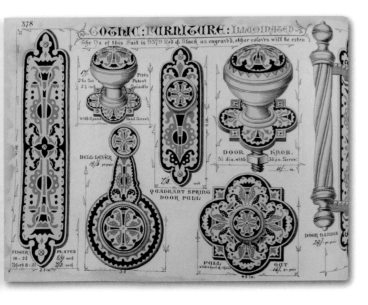

The endpapers of technical manuals of the 1890s advertised an impressive range of cheap instruction books.

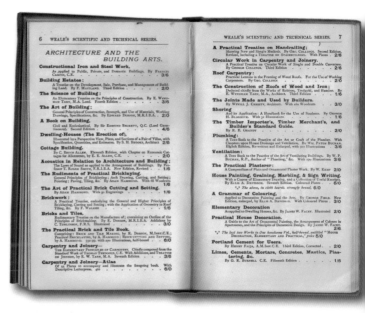

In speculative suburbs, this approach was reversed. Streets were laid out to accommodate the greatest number of houses, regardless of topography. Mains water, gas, sewers, and eventually electricity made orientation irrelevant. Building Acts prescribed the dimensions and materials of the house without reference to individual occupants. Working drawings became more accurate and detailed, and no variation from the plans was permitted.

Industrialisation meant that bricks and other materials were mass-produced in standard shapes and sizes and carried by canal or rail throughout the country. The consequent loss of local architectural character was inevitable: without mass production, division of labour and standardisation, it would have been impossible to meet the demand for new housing.

Loudon observed that chimney flues were no longer pargeted (lined) in the old-fashioned way, with loam and cow-dung: 'quicklime and pounded brick are found far better, and are now generally used by the best London builders.' Fifty years later, the carpenter Walter Rose saw the imported term 'bricklayer' supersede 'masoner', the old dialect name for a builder: 'to the villager the bricklayer was an aristocrat of the craft, and belonged to the life of towns'. The citified construction industry had broken its old connection with rural building crafts.

Some regional traditions persisted. The fine stonework found throughout the suburbs of Bristol, and Reading's distinctive silvery-grey bricks are examples of local building materials that preserved a regional flavour in standardised housing.

Opposite top left: Finely carved decorative stonework is a feature of even modest houses in the suburbs of Bristol. This example in Clifton incorporates scenes from Aesop's fables in the panels around the windows.

Opposite top right and bottom: Terraced housing of the 1870s in Reading built with local silver-coloured brick.

SUBURBAN DEVELOPMENT

THE LEASEHOLD SYSTEM that underpinned the development of English suburbs was devised for building the great estates of Georgian London. As the city expanded and demand for housing grew, owners of land on the edges of the built-up area would offer building leases to developers, on plots laid out around an infrastructure of roads, sewers and a place of worship.

Surveyors specified the dimensions, materials and workmanship to be used in building the houses, and approved the finished appearance of the street frontage. Standards and sizes varied from the 'first-rate' houses on the main thoroughfares to the mews and commercial premises on the side streets. If not controlled, the land behind would be covered with 'jerry-built' houses, some only 12 feet wide, which would quickly deteriorate and drag the neighbourhood down.

Where demand for housing was most acute, for example in the industrial North in the early nineteenth century, landowners could find contractors willing to buy leases as short as twenty years. Friedrich Engels, visiting Manchester in 1842, was appalled by the consequences of frenzied development. The neat appearance of the newly built 'back-to-back' houses for cotton workers was 'a pretence which vanishes within the first ten years ... on closer examination, it becomes evident that the walls of these cottages are as thin as it is possible to make them.' Engels blamed these ready-made slums on greedy contractors exploiting a leasehold system that made it uneconomical to build and maintain working-men's cottages for longer than forty years.

Few developers could fund the development of an entire estate, so they would add a link to the chain of credit by selling sub-leases to several builders, requiring each to build perhaps a single terrace or a handful of houses. The builders raised *their* capital on under-leases. In boom times, many small investors were tempted to put money into local building enterprises. J. W. Papworth wrote in 1857 that an investor 'need not be a builder, or a tradesman in any branch of building: indeed, the persons whom I have known succeed best, were a sailor ... and a footman.' Leases were an efficient

Opposite: New housing under construction for lower middle-class families in Peckham, South London, at the dawn of the twentieth century. The bricklayers have completed the chimneystacks and set the pots on top, and the front-facing roof gables are nearly finished. In the foreground are the footings for the houses that will soon be built on the opposite side of the street, with floor timbers stacked ready for use.

Belgrave Square, built in the mid-1820s by Cubitt to designs by the architect George Basevi (1794–1845), set a standard for first-class terraced housing that would prevail for the next forty years. An early image shows the north-east side with workmen in the foreground preparing the roadway for an asphalt finish.

method of raising capital and spreading risk on large-scale developments, but the economic benefits were clustered at the top of the chain and bankruptcies were common among small builders. When a firm failed, creditors might perforce become 'builders', and take over a half-finished project in order to salvage something of their investment.

The model and inspiration for many Victorian builders was Thomas Cubitt (1788–1855), the contractor (he preferred 'builder') who developed Belgravia under the leasehold system in collaboration with the Grosvenor Estate. The son of a Norfolk carpenter, Cubitt earned his set-up capital working as a ship's carpenter, and was lucky enough to start his firm during a building boom in the 1820s.

Cubitt's genius was organisational: he excelled at co-ordinating surveyors, architects and other developers in complex projects. Instead of subcontracting non-carpentry work, he employed his own workforce encompassing all the building trades. Crucially, the scale and ambition of his operations enabled him to retain the confidence of investors through the economic troughs and peaks that affected the building industry.

Belgravia, begun in the mid-1820s and completed after Cubitt's death, illustrates the leasehold system at its best. The site was unpromising – a clayey swamp – but the location was perfect to meet the demand for genteel housing west of central London.

Grosvenor's building lease obliged Cubitt to drain the land, provide sewers, roads and pavements, and to construct Belgrave Square and its associated streets and mews. Cubitt shared the financial risk with a consortium of wealthy investors, and the workload with other contractors. The development was designed to attract wealth, as James Elmes noted in 1827:

> This extensive area is now covering with mansions and handsome houses ... destined to be the future residences of the highest class of the fashionable world .... The streets and square are paved, Macadamised and lighted, on the most approved principles; the houses are constructed with the best materials.

Cubitt later built Pimlico – modest squares and streets built by smaller firms to his specifications – on Grosvenor land between Belgravia and the Thames. His firm eventually had a vast depot on the riverbank, receiving Portland stone slabs, slates from north Wales, and materials from their own brickworks, foundry, sawmill and cement works. They had a professional staff of architects and surveyors, and their own legal and letting departments. Cubitt achieved fame, moved in the highest circles (he collaborated with the Prince Consort on royal residences and the 1851 Great Exhibition), and left an estate worth over £1 million.

General contractors were more likely to succeed if they worked at the top end of the market, had a sufficient spread of activities to redeploy men during slumps, and conducted their business with ruthless efficiency: in Summerson's description, the successful Victorian builder was 'no remote board-room personage. If he was to survive he had to face his men, command them and, if necessary, endure their hatred.'

Not every developer could be a Cubitt, nor every suburb as grand as Belgravia. However, there were enough success stories for the social ascent of the prosperous suburban

The suburban paterfamilias struggling with the upkeep of a defective house was one of *Punch* magazine's stock figures of fun and was the inspiration for Mr Pooter in *The Diary of a Nobody*. Here, cracks are appearing in the render before the adjoining house is finished.

contractor to become a subject for ridicule. In George Grossmith's *Diary of a Nobody* (1892), Pooter the clerk is thrilled to attend the Lord Mayor's Ball but discomfited to find his jobbing builder among the other guests:

A terraced
street with a
building break
illustrates
adherence
to a general
specification but
a change of detail
where one set of
houses ended and
another began.

> He said, in the most familiar way: 'This is better than Brickfield Terrace, eh?' I simply looked at him, and said coolly: 'I never expected to see you here.' He said, with a loud, coarse laugh: 'I like that—if YOU, why not ME?' ... I said, by way of reproof to him: 'You never sent to-day to paint the bath, as I requested.' Farmerson said: 'Pardon me, Mr. Pooter, no shop when we're in company, please.'

Before I could think of a reply, one of the sheriffs, in full Court costume, slapped Farmerson on the back and hailed him as an old friend, and asked him to dine with him at his lodge. I was astonished ... 'To think that a man who mends our scraper should know any member of our aristocracy!'

t is hard to establish how many people worked in the Victorian building industry. Its reliance on human muscle power demanded a large labour force, but even so, according to the *Building News* in 1866, most firms employed fewer than ten men. Many of the 23,515 'employers of carpenters, joiners, bricklayers, masons and plasterers' recorded in England and Wales in the 1851 census were self-employed. The number doubled to 46,973 by 1891, and about half of these were self-employed. The 1861 census listed 3,845 builders in London, whereas Kelly's *Directory* for the same year has only 1,766 (but states business addresses and may therefore give a more accurate picture). In Bristol, there were 141 'builders' in 1825, and 351 in 1885, but there were slumps from the mid-1850s to the 1860s and again in the 1890s. To set up as a builder was a gamble, and most firms lasted less than ten years.

Contractors typically built a few houses at a time within the freeholder's overall plan and specification. Most building firms in late-Victorian London produced fewer than six houses a year outside the boom years of the 1880s; only the very largest firms built houses by the hundred (one such was Watts of Catford, who achieved four hundred houses a year in the 1890s).

Masters, men and apprentices pose in front of a half-finished street of houses in Bristol. A 'For Sale' sign attests to the developer's need to sell the properties as soon as possible and move on to the next project. New owners were equally keen to take possession, and many residents of new suburbs waited months for their streets to be paved and lit after they had moved in.

HOUSE DESIGNS

The main influences on the design of Victorian middle-class housing were legislation and regulation, changes in the architectural profession, and mass production of materials.

The London Building Act 1774 consolidated previous building regulations, standardised different 'rates' of housing and was a model for subsequent legislation, providing a template for specifying house dimensions and building standards for suburban terraced housing that would persist until the First World War.

The nineteenth century witnessed a proliferation of Building Acts. Municipal authorities added layers of local bye-laws and began to administer their own systems of building control through borough surveyors, engineers

Opposite:
The daughter of the house stands proudly in front of a classic halls-adjoining semi, in about 1900. Clever design could make such houses look bigger than they really were: at first glance, the shared gable and continuous lintel over both front doors gives the impression of a single, rather grand dwelling, but at close range the demarcation of private territory through railings and separate porches becomes clear.

Left:
A 'Queen Anne' house of the mid-1870s in Bedford Park, West London, an influential 'garden suburb' for the artistic middle classes. This is an early example of the use of attractive perspective views to advertise speculative developments.

Right:
The description
of a house as
'fourth-rate' did
not mean that
it was built to
a poor standard,
but that it adhered
to the specification
laid down in
legislation for
the smallest
class of terraced
housing, as shown
in J. D. Simon's
*House-Owner's
Estimator* (1881).
Fourth-rate houses
were the typical
'two up, two down'
cottages of
the Victorian
working-class
suburb.

Far right: Within
the standard
specification
there was some
scope for variation:
in this fourth-rate
terrace in Bethnal
Green, East
London, the
ground-floor
windows have
decorative
cast-iron mullions
and the doors are
framed in glazed
bullnose brick.

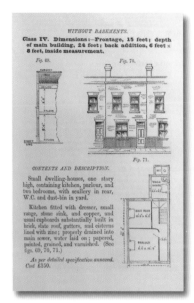

and public health officers. These measures improved structural safety,
sanitation and fire prevention, and house planning.

Improved standards increased building costs, until speculative builders
could not build cheaply enough to meet demand for working-class housing and
were exclusively catering for the middle market. Philanthropic organisations
such as the Peabody Trust and the Improved Industrial Dwellings Company
attempted to fill the gap. By the 1880s, however, lack of decent cheap housing
forced local authorities to provide working-class accommodation. The London
County Council inaugurated its first estate in 1890, replacing the notorious
Old Nichol slum with blocks of Arts-and-Crafts flats at Boundary Road,
Bethnal Green.

A second influence on mass-market house design was the absence
of professional architects. Seeking to assert their professional status as
specialists with theoretical and technical knowledge that distinguished them
from tradesman-builders (the Royal Institution of British Architects
was incorporated in 1834), architects largely removed themselves
from speculative development, leaving contractors to obtain designs for
mass-market houses elsewhere. So builders turned to pattern books and
professional journals for suggestions for dressing their houses with the
superficial features of fashionable architectural styles. For architectural
theorists such as A. W. N. Pugin (1812–52) and John Ruskin (1819–1900)
the creativity of the craftsman-builder and the touch of the human hand were
essential to true Gothic or Arts-and-Crafts architecture, but their views were

irrelevant to the average builder, for whom style – whether rusticated render used as Classical shorthand in the 1840s, polychrome brick representing mid-century 'Gothic', or red-brick 'Queen Anne' in the 1870s – was purely a means of appealing to potential purchasers.

Although unwilling to provide designs, architects did not hesitate to criticise 'the ordinary class of suburban "Speculation Villas"' in which the internal arrangement was left to the builder, so that, Robert Kerr complained in *The Gentleman's House* (1864), 'a Kitchen doorway in the Vestibule or Staircase exposes to the view of every one the dresser or the cooking-range, or fills the house with unwelcome odours.'

Above: The Improved General Dwellings Company provided affordable working-class housing at a modest profit for investors. Pre-cast cement window surrounds and cast-iron structural elements helped to keep construction costs down.

Left: A key precept of the Gothic Revival was that decoration should be incorporated into buildings via their structural materials. In this North Oxford house of the 1860s, bands of coloured brick contrast with the stone window surrounds and the window arch contains some distinctive herringbone patterned brickwork.

Mass-production made it easier and cheaper to adopt the latest fashions. As the *Building News* commented in 1896, suburban houses could

The oversupply of middle-class housing towards the end of the nineteenth century encouraged speculative builders to tempt potential buyers with fashionable 'old English' decorative details. Here, the embellishments include tile-hanging, pebbledash, complex joinery and even a castellated parapet to the window bay.

… be built cheaper and quicker if the same plans and templates, window-frames and sashes, the same stone dressings, the same fastenings and ironmongery are used, than if each of these things undergoes modification to suit individual taste ….The builder knows exactly the width and number of bricks and closers required for each pier; he can tell the number of bricks required for each house; he can order ornamental stringcourses and cornices wholesale, as he can his iron guttering and his railing … multiplication of the same details and fittings enables a considerable reduction to be made in the cost of erecting a few hundreds of houses.

Towards 1900, the oversupply of middle-class housing led developers to load their houses with seductive features, and quite modest houses were embellished with geometric tiled paths, glazed porch dados, fretwork valances, stained glass panels and cast-iron finials.

ON SITE

Each workman on a building site had his own place in a hierarchy determined partly by his trade, but mostly by his level of skill. The nature of the work counted for less than seniority in the job, as pay rates were similar across all the trades. Master craftsmen were the senior workers, sufficiently well established in their respective trades to employ others as journeymen, and take on apprentices.

Training began with humble tasks: carpenters would start off sweeping the workshop and tending the glue pot. Practical training was supplemented by formal study of relevant subjects such as geometry or draughtsmanship. As an apprentice carpenter Walter Rose attended weekly evening classes for two years, walking seven miles there and back in the dark (during winter, so as not to lose work during the long summer days). Another way for apprentices to broaden their education was a period of 'improvership' in a different branch of the trade: Rose's brother was 'improved' in London, experiencing the continuous construction of identical houses in contrast to the varied and seasonal work available in the village.

A bright and willing apprentice could progress quickly: a training begun at fourteen years of age could see a young man on half wages at nineteen, and ready to earn an independent living as a time-served craftsman by his twenty-first birthday. He then became a journeyman, qualified to work independently for an agreed daily wage.

The foreman was a craftsman whose organisational ability and force of character had earned him promotion to a managerial position. He measured up the work, calculated costs and prepared tenders. It was essential to agree costs 'very plainly in writing' before starting work, Kerr advised, adding, 'there is no exception to this rule, except where the works consist of mere jobbing; and even then no gentleman need be ashamed to ask the builder for a written memorandum of description and estimate.' There were two accepted methods of pricing. A day-bill was based on time and materials charged at a standard profit of 15 per cent. Kerr disliked this method, which allowed builders to exaggerate the

A carefully composed photograph of builders on a housing development towards the end of the nineteenth century. The men display the emblems of their trades, including trowels and hods for the bricklayers, saws and a plane for the carpenters, and a hawk (mortar board) and loose-tined rake for the plasterers. The painters and decorators wear white, and one of them holds a large distemper brush. They have nearly completed four pairs of identical, semi-detached houses and have put the footings in place for the next pair, on the right-hand side behind the stout gentleman with the proprietorial air – surely the master builder himself. The presence of so many trades on site reflects the overlapping sequence of activities necessary to keep the houses coming.

cost of materials and time spent. He preferred 'Measure and Value' (quantity surveying).

Bullying and threats of dismissal were commonly used to keep employees in line. 'Old Misery', the foreman on Tressell's fictional building site, is a petty despot, spying on his men to catch them slacking, and demoralising them by insisting they 'scamp' work to save costs. He is ready to 'square or bluff' (bribe or persuade) surveyors and supervising architects to approve shoddy work. Having been a journeyman 'on the point of starting on his own account', he becomes foreman for 'two pounds a week, and two-and-a-half per cent of the profits'. In choosing security over independence he loses the autonomy of the master-craftsman, and realises too late that his dedication to the business has been all for the owner's benefit.

Unskilled labourers, who spent their working lives fetching and carrying for the craftsmen, provided most of the raw muscle power on site. Without education or training, they had little prospect of advancement, and faced destitution when injury or old age prevented them from continuing hard physical labour.

EXCAVATION

The first stage of construction was excavation. This was done manually, by labourers using crowbars, picks and shovels, and was supervised by the bricklayer, who provided the tools. A typical schedule of 'Excavator's,

The only way to house the population of the capital, which grew from 2,235,000 in 1841 to 6,581,000 in 1901, was to keep building: here, a forest of scaffold poles on a site next to an already dense development indicates the onward march of the South London suburbs, in streets of three-storey terraced houses intended for professional middle-class commuters.

'Well digger's and Bricklayer's work' of the 1830s included digging the basement and trenches for the foundations, then 'punning' the bottom and sides of the excavations with a rammer to provide a firm base. Excavated earth was used to form gradients and levels for the surrounding paths and roads.

The cost was estimated by the cubic yard of excavated material. Since every lump of earth was removed by hand, using baskets and wheelbarrows, even the distance that loaded barrows had to be wheeled across site to reach the carter's wagon was separately priced, per 'run' of 20 yards.

Large excavations needed coffer-dams to support their sides, and pumps to remove ground-water. This required 'labourers of a superior class, accustomed to the management of pile-engines and tackle, and competent to the execution of such rough carpenter's work as is required in timbering.'

Many early-Victorian developments had no mains water or sewers, so excavations included wells and cesspits. Wells were priced per foot depth, and had to be 'steined' (lined with brick or stone) – a dangerous job for the bricklayer, who sat on a plank to be lowered into the shaft to complete his work.

SCAFFOLDING

Bricklayers were also responsible for scaffolding. This was made from softwood poles lashed together with ropes, with wedges driven into the lashings to tighten them. 'Standards' were well-seasoned timber poles, 6–7 inches in diameter, bedded directly into the ground. Horizontal members or 'ledgers'

Builders in Peckham, East London, c. 1880–90. The scaffolding of poles lashed together with rope is designed for access, with little regard for the safety of the men, who needed agility and a head for heights in order to carry out their work.

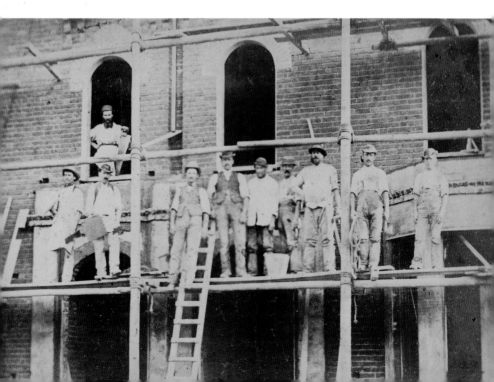

were lashed to the standards and held to the wall by 'putlogs' of birchwood, one end of which rested in the wall until the scaffold was dismantled – at which point the void where the putlog had rested was filled with brick to match the surrounding wall. The putlogs supported the scaffold boards, thick timbers bound at each end with an iron hoop to prevent them from splitting. They could not be used in ashlar (smooth stonework) walls; in such cases a free-standing scaffold was supported by two rows of standards.

Many scaffolders were former sailors, who were accustomed to climbing rigging and working at height, and could tie knots that would guarantee the safety of all the workmen. When designing a scaffold, claimed one writer, 'it will be found that … half an hour with an expert scaffolder … preferably an old sailor, will afford more instruction than hours spent in studying diagrams'. A scaffold might be reconfigured as work progressed, according to the requirements of the job. It would not be struck until the external walls and chimney stacks were finished.

BRICKLAYING

Bricklayers photographed in Manchester in 1900 as they complete the chimney breast and internal walls of a bedroom. A plumb rule leans against the wall behind the man on the left. The patchy appearance of the internal walls contrasts with the 'fair face' brickwork of the neighbour's gable but is not necessarily evidence of poor workmanship: as long as the walls were true, and soundly built, defects in their appearance were acceptable because they would be hidden by the plaster finish.

The foundations completed, the bricklayer's labourer started mixing mortar and sorting bricks. In the early nineteenth century, in areas where brick earth (clay) was readily available, the bricks might be made on the spot, using material dug out of the basement and fired in makeshift kilns or 'clamps'. The growth of the brickmaking industry and improved transport made high-quality, uniform bricks widely available in a great variety of colours and shapes.

Mortar, a mix of slaked lime and sand, was made in advance and allowed to mature for as long as possible before being 'knocked up' (chopped and mixed with a spade) to make it workable. This was a laborious job that could not be skimped, because it improved the mortar's plasticity and adhesive properties. A mix of the wrong consistency would immediately be rejected by the bricklayer.

The labourer carried bricks and mortar in batches where they were needed, keeping up an unbroken flow of materials to support his master's working rhythm. The pair would move round the building to ensure that no 'lift' or section of new wall exceeded 4 feet per day; this allowed the mortar to dry and the brickwork to settle before the next day's work. Apprentice bricklayers began by building interior walls, where defects in their work would be concealed by plaster, before they were allowed to tackle 'fair-face' brickwork. A skilled bricklayer was expected to lay about 1,000 bricks of plain walling (3 cubic yards) per day, extra time and money being allowed for arches, corbelling and other specialist work.

The bricklayer provided walls and chimney stacks with fireplace openings; he built enclosures for laundry coppers, and laid brick paving to lightwells, cellars and passages. Drain and sewer pipes, traps and inspection chambers, and tiled floors for kitchens, sculleries and pantries also came within his remit.

Bricklayers' mates loading hods in front of a half-finished terrace. Building regulations required timber sash boxes to be concealed within the brickwork, so bricklayers' work had to be synchronised with that of the carpenters. Timber elements made in the carpenters' workshop were brought to the site as needed: to the left in this image is a stack of ready-made sash boxes awaiting insertion.

An arch
composed of
rubbed brickwork,
so called because
the fine-grained red
bricks were
abraded to
fit together so
precisely that they
were practically
self-supporting,
needing only a
thin smear of
pure lime putty
to join them. This
example is from
East Malling, Kent.

The problem of
what to do with
the blank gable
wall at the end
of a terrace is
solved in this
example of 1885
in Osney, Oxford,
using the simplest
of materials – two
colours of brick,
with headers
(the ends) and
stretchers (the
sides) organised in
patterned bands.
The figure '5'
in the date
has caused
the bricklayer
some difficulty.

Panels of carved brick or moulded terracotta with Japanese-influenced Aesthetic decoration, particularly vases of sunflowers, were widely used in the 1880s.

Working outdoors in a 'wet trade' caused arthritis in the hands, and bricklayers suffered from 'bricklayer's itch', a skin disease caused by the drying effect of alkaline lime mortar. Lime could also damage eyes, either from accidental burns or through conjunctivitis caused by lime dust.

A handbook of 1894 listed the bricklayer's tools:

> ... the *trowel*, to take up and spread the mortar, and to cut bricks to the requisite length; the *brick axe*, for shaping bricks to any required bevel; the *tin saw*, for making incisions in brick to be cut with the axe, and a *rubbing-stone*, on which to rub the bricks smooth after being roughly axed into shape. The *jointer* and the *jointing-rule* are used for running the centres of the mortar-joints. The *raker* for raking out the mortar from the joints of old brickwork previous to re-pointing. The *hammer*, for cutting chasings and splays.

A square, a level and a plumbline were used to keep the work true, and gauge-rods to ensure that the brick courses lined up with elements such as stone cills. A table called a 'banker' – the same name as that given to a stonemason's workbench – was used for trial assembly of complex elements.

By exploiting the geometrical possibilities of brick headers and stretchers (short and long sides) and all the naturally occurring clay colours, bricklayers could create an infinity of patterns. 'Polychromatic', or multi-coloured, brickwork became fashionable as a result of Gothic revival architects' insistence on 'honest' building, in which constructional materials were not hidden under render and stucco but revealed and celebrated, their intrinsic texture, shape and colour used to provide visual interest.

The 1860s was the high point of the fashion for polychromy. A different aspect of the bricklayer's art

The 1897 edition of the *Contractor's Compendium* carried this advertisement, which shows the range of ready-made clay products available to builders. Besides bricks and tiles, dragon finials, crested ridge tiles, balustrades and vases were also on offer.

Tools and
techniques
to reduce the
effort of moving
heavy pieces of
stone included
various forms of
lewis – simple 'crab'
pincers that use the
weight of the stone
as it is lifted to
tighten their hold.
A triple lewis was
known as 'St Peter's
keys' in honour of
the patron saint
of stonemasons.

came to the fore in the 1870s, when 'Queen Anne' architects such as Richard
Norman Shaw (1831–1912) led the fashion for red-brick houses with
decorative moulded courses, carved 'aprons' below windows, and terracotta
panels moulded with Japanese motifs or sunflowers. Side and back walls
were often built in cheaper stock brick without any decoration; hence the
disparaging description, 'Queen Anne in front, Mary Anne behind'.

MASONRY

The use of stone has usually denoted a high-status building, but even humble
cottages incorporated stone window sills or doorsteps, so stonemasons
worked closely with bricklayers. They were assisted by stonecutters, who took
delivery of large stones from the quarry and cut them into blocks of roughly
the right shape and size for working into their final form.

The mason produced finished pieces by chiselling 'draughts' (lines
corresponding roughly to the required shape) and knocking off the waste
stone between them. Bevelled or rebated edges would be achieved using
'squares' made from two wood scantlings nailed together at the required
angle. For mouldings, a zinc sheet cut and filed to the desired profile was
repeatedly held up to the block to ensure the accuracy of the work in
progress. The finished piece was smoothed by rubbing with sand, or in the
case of a hard stone, a 'drag' – a hard edge of steel with an indented edge that
filed the surface of the stone to a smooth face.

The mason exploited different stones for particular functions or visual
effects. Hard or grainy stones were 'fair-tooled' (with the marks of the chisel
aligned in a discernible pattern), 'random-tooled', or 'boasted' (rough-hewn

The blank window
surround (left)
on the entrance
front of Oxford
University Museum
indicates where
the decorative
carving was
to have been
done *in situ;* the
intended finish
to this window
can be seen in
the window
on the right.

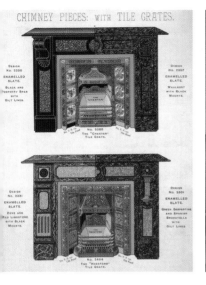

CHIMNEY PIECES: WITH TILE GRATES.

Far left:
Jesse Sessions
& Co, builders'
merchants based in
Gloucester Docks,
specialised in
'enamelling' slate
chimneypieces with
imitation marble
finishes. They
processed slate
brought by boat
from Wales, and
sent the finished
items out on the
canals and railways
that radiated out
from Gloucester.
A catalogue page
depicts a choice
of four patterns
of enamelled
chimneypiece
on two fireplace
illustrations.

Above right:
Is this chimneypiece
in a late-Victorian
terraced house in
Hackney real
marble, or
enamelled slate?
The quality of
the professional
marbling made it
impossible to tell
the difference,
except at very
close range.
The impressive
mirror surround
is a subsequent
addition.

with a broad chisel). The exposed face of the hardest granites and gritstones would be left as hewn from the quarry, with the marks of the 'scappling hammer' or stone-axe.

Nineteenth-century specifications for mason's work typically include York stone steps, paving, sinks and hearths, Portland stone or milled slate shelves for wine cellars, pantries and dairies, and marble or Portland stone chimneypieces. The exterior of a Classical house would have a crisp Portland stone cornice, while a Gothic house required window mullions and drip moulds of mellow Bath stone. From about 1840, steam-driven machines were used to process quarried stone into standardised shapes.

Master masons were educated in geometry and mathematics so that they could set out three-dimensional work accurately and calculate materials and prices – stone being the most expensive building material, and the least likely to be adaptable for use on another job if over-ordered. Large block masonry was charged for by the cubic foot; cornices, lintels and sills by the linear foot; paving less than 3 inches thick by the square foot. Different piece rates were used according to the hardness of the stone and the difficulty of working it, from marble and granite (the hardest) through Purbeck, York and Derbyshire grit, to Portland and Bath, which were the easiest to work.

Decorative carving was a separate, highly respected, branch of stonemasonry whose practitioners were insistent on their status as skilled specialists. Thomas Hardy described the provincial hero of *Jude the Obscure* (1895) as 'a handy man at his trade, an all-round man, as artizans in country-towns are apt to be,' unlike his London counterpart, 'who carves the boss or knob of leafage [but] declines to cut the fragment of moulding which merges in that leafage, as if it were a degradation to do the second half of one whole.'

CARPENTRY AND JOINERY

Edward Dobson, writing in the 1890s, made a simple distinction between carpentry and joinery: 'The work of the carpenter does not require the use of the plane, which is one of the principal tools of the joiner ... the carpenter being engaged in the rough framework, and the joiner on the finishing and decorations of buildings.' In practice, however, the trades overlapped. Moreover, the terms 'carpenter' and 'builder' were interchangeable because so many building firms were started by ambitious carpenters: involved in every building operation, they were best placed to understand the sequence and co-ordination of all the trades.

Items listed in an early-Victorian description of 'carpenter's work' are those concealed by decorative finishes – wall plates, joists, roof timbers and troughs for lead-lined gutters – while internal structure and finishes are assigned to the joiner. The latter include 'straight inch [thick] floors with proper borders to [hearth] slabs in the parlour, passage and bed-rooms' panelled internal doors; frames architraves, mouldings, linings and skirtings; the windows and the staircase. The specification ends with a catch-all clause requiring the joiner to 'prepare and fix all manner of beads, stops, fillets, grounds, linings and backings required for the perfect execution of the work'.

Woodworkers had to use 'best well-seasoned yellow deal (kept till so dry as to be in no danger of shrinking when used), free from sap and shakes', and 'find all the materials, tools, labour, nails, glue, and every description of iron-mongery, locks, bolts, bars, hinges, and fastenings, and the carriage and fixing thereof.'

Large firms selected the raw timber, converted it into planks, beams and boards, and seasoned it in their own timber yards. The rule of thumb was one year's seasoning per inch thickness of timber, so buying

A detailed drawing of a window in a builder's handbook of about 1855 depicts every element of the joinery for a bay window, including the box shutters and the sash weights.

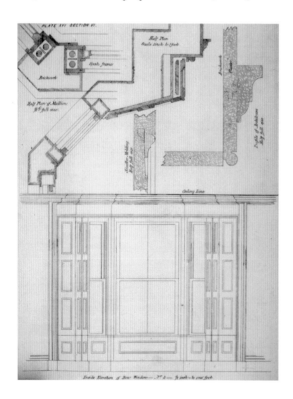

imber years in advance was essential to the continuity of a business. Walter Rose's grandfather could obtain English oak, ash and elm from the local woods but for deal he travelled from rural Buckinghamshire to the canal wharf at Uxbridge to choose from imported logs still floating in the water. It was not until the mid-1880s that timber merchants' sales reps started to travel into the Chilterns.

In 1843, 1,317,645 loads of timber (cut and uncut) were brought into English ports. By 1857, the figure had almost doubled, at 2,495,964 loads, and by 1866 it had increased again, to 3,638,344 loads. 53,458 tons of mahogany were brought into the country in 1866. Not all this timber was for the construction industry, but certainly most of the imported Baltic deal went into buildings, as English pine was not strong enough for structural uses.

Logs were converted into planks by two-man teams of sawyers in a sawpit. The work was strenuous, dirty and potentially dangerous. 'Who would be a Sawyer? Or, being one, would not work out his own reformation in time?' asked Nathaniel Whittock, in 1837.

Above:
The cover of a timber merchant's catalogue of about 1900 depicts a depot with a steam-powered sawmill, board and deal warehouses, drying yards and its own railway sidings.

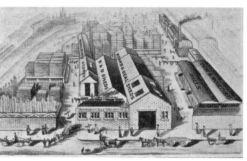

Left:
Mechanisation increased the choice and brought down the price of ready-made timber elements.

Balusters.

Prices per dozen. All 3 feet long, with 22 ins. of turning; 5 in. top; 9 in. bottom square.

Nos.	Thickness	Deal.	Pitch Pine.	Oak.	Wainscot or Walnut.	Nos.	Thickness	Deal.	Pitch Pine.	Nos.	Thickness	Deal.	Pitch Pine.	Oak.	Wainscot or Walnut.
19 & 20	1½ ins.	5/4	8/8	10/-	13/4	43	2 ins.	10/8		46	2 ins.	9/-	15/4	—	—
,, ,,	2 ,,	8/-	12/-	15/4	20/-	44	1½ ,,	3/4	7/4	47	2 ,,	17/4	21/4	37/4	42/8
21	1¼ ,,	6/-	9/4	10/8	14/-	,,	*1¾ ,,	4/4	9/4	48 & 49	2 ,,	20/-	24/-	40/-	45/4
,,	2 ,,	8/8	12/8	16/-	20/8	,,	2 ,,	5/8	11/4	50	2 ,,	22/-	26/-	42/8	48/-
22 & 23	1½ ,,	15/4	17/4	17/4	20/-	45	1½ ,,	6/-	10/-	51	2 ,,	23/4	27/4	45/4	50/8
,,	2 ,,	18/8	22/8	24/8	26/8	,,	1¾ ,,	7/-	12/-	52	1½ ,,	4/8	8/-	—	—
24	2 ,,	20/-	24/-	—	—	,,	2 ,,	8/4	14/8	,,	1½ ,,	6/-	9/8	—	—
43	1½ ,,	3/-	6/8	—	—	46	1½ ,,	6/8	10/8	,,	2 ,,	7/4	11/4	—	—
,,	1¾ ,,	4/-	8/8	—	—	,,	1¾ ,,	7/8	12/8						

BRISTOL

WICKHAM & NORRIS.

Steam power transformed the industry so that by the 1880s, timber merchants were supplying machine-planed planks and boards. Rose never heard a sawyer complain about his work being taken over by machines, and he did not miss hand-planing, 'a monotonous hard job formerly held to be a punishment task for refractory apprentices'.

The woodwork for a new house started with the exterior door frames which went in as soon as the foundations were finished. As the walls rose, the carpenter divided his time between site and workshop. On site, he supplied the bricklayer with formers to support arches under construction, bond timbers, and oak 'bricks' for building into walls alongside door and window openings to provide fixing points for timber mouldings. At the workshop he made all the interior elements, ready to go in as soon as the walls were finished. The making of a simple four-panelled door was considered a days work for a trained carpenter; constructing a sash window took longer but was more satisfying because of the precision it required. Timesheets were kept but were not the only evidence of work completed: when apprentices swept the workshop before the foreman's rounds, carpenters would shoo them away from the benches to preserve the piles of shavings that showed how much had been accomplished that day.

Floor joists had to go in quickly because the bricklayers were waiting to proceed upward. Another deadline was the completion of the walls, by which time all the ready-made joinery had to be delivered. Once they had completed the roof structure, the carpenters worked continuously on 'fixing – installing floors, doorframes, skirtings and other mouldings, and lastly hanging the doors and windows, with their ironmongery.

ROOFING

Tile, slate, lead and thatch roof coverings were provided by different tradesmen, and the introduction from France of asphalt roofing in the 1830s called for yet another set of skills. Traditionally, roof coverings reflected locally available materials: clay tiles in London and the south-east, thatch in East Anglia, green slates in Westmorland, and honey-coloured Cotswold stone slabs. During the nineteenth century, however, Welsh slate – cheap, easy to work and readily available via canal and railway – became ubiquitous in speculative housing.

The characteristic tool of the slater was the 'zax' or 'saixe', a hatchet with a sharp point at the back used for trimming slates and making two holes in each for the fixing nails. Rustproof copper or zinc nails were used until the mid-century, when galvanised nails became available.

Traditionally, slates had been laid in progressively smaller sizes ascending course by course to the ridge, but in speculative housing it was easier and cheaper to provide the same size throughout a development

The Arts-and-Crafts flats of the Boundary Estate in Bethnal Green have roofs of Westmorland slate laid in the traditional manner, with diminishing courses.

Consequently many suburbs had rather monotonous roofscapes of blue-grey slate with clay ridge tiles. Towards the end of the century, some traditional building practices were revived by Arts-and-Crafts architects: blocks of early LCC flats have distinctive Westmorland slate roofs laid in diminishing courses.

Each size of slate had a name: between the small 'singles' and 'doubles' (1ft 1in x 6in) and the largest 'rags' or 'imperials' (2ft 6in x 2ft) were 'ladies', 'countesses' and 'duchesses'. Special sizes and shapes to cover valleys and hips had to be riven (split) or cut on site. The slater also dealt with items made from sawn slate, such as chimneypieces, cisterns, and larder shelves – for which polished slate provided an ideal wipeable surface.

PLASTERING

Plasterers were responsible for external render, plain or with incisions or decorative mouldings that imitated ashlar or decorative carving. Inside the house, they had to 'lath, lay, set and white' the walls and ceilings: that is, install a screen of laths to support three, progressively smoother, layers of plaster, and finish the job with a coat of limewash.

Plaster was lime putty mixed with various additives. External render gave rough brickwork a protective coat that could be made to look like ashlar, so sand was added to strengthen the mix, increase its weather-resistance and give it a grainy stone texture. The render to the lower floors might be scored, to enhance the illusion of stone blocks, or rusticated – built up around wooden battens that were removed once the render was dry, leaving channels that looked like deep joints between 'stones'.

Internal walls were covered with three layers of plaster. Animal hair was added to make 'coarse stuff' for the first layer. Ox hair was preferred. It came from farms and slaughterhouses, and there was a slight risk that it

The first coat of plaster is applied to the laths, while the plasterer's labourer readies the next batch. Laths were made of oak, chestnut or pine; machine-sawn laths were cheaper but split or 'riven' laths provided better grip.

Below left: A cartoon by Everard Hopkins depicts a house with the bare bricks of the chimneybreast and the laths on the partition wall ready for plastering.

Below right: Bundles of laths leaning against a newly-lathed wall in a Victorian house restoration project, 2010.

carried tetanus or anthrax. The hair was added just before the plaster was used because long exposure to wet lime would cause the fibre to disintegrate. It was mixed in using a 'drag', a rake with three tines widely spaced so as not to become clogged.

The flat surfaces of walls and ceilings were made by pressing the 'coarse stuff' onto the laths so that it oozed through the gaps and spread out over the back of the laths. The plaster as it dried became firmly hooked onto the laths and provided a base for the following coats.

Plastering flat walls and ceilings remained a laborious, messy job until the widespread adoption of plasterboard after the Second World War, but during the nineteenth century decorative relief plasterwork moved off site and into the workshop, as new materials and methods made obsolete the old techniques of moulding wet plaster *in situ*, and mechanical substitutes were found for the skills of the freehand modeller.

The basis for most plaster cornices was a straight-run moulding applied directly to the wall or ceiling using a profile mounted or 'horsed' on a wooden frame that held it rigid. In the early Victorian period the profile was made of close-grained hardwood such as box or pear. These were superseded by zinc, which was lighter and damp-resistant.

Additional decorative details or 'enrichments' were cast separately in moulds of hardwood or wax and fixed into place with dabs of plaster of Paris. From about 1850 the use of gelatine moulds became widespread. These were flexible, so could be used for undercut details that could not be achieved using

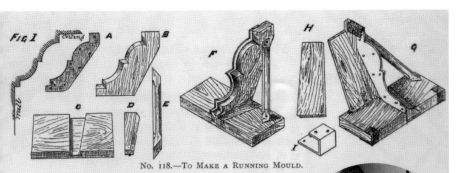

NO. 118.—TO MAKE A RUNNING MOULD.

moulds made from the old, rigid materials. The flexibility also made it easier to release the cast item without damage, so fewer castings were spoilt. Gelatine moulds did not last as long as those of wood or wax, but were durable enough: in 1871 the plasterers Millar of Glasgow produced 125 clean casts from a single gelatine cornice mould.

Alternative materials for enrichments were *papier-mâché* or 'carton pierre', which were lighter than solid plaster, and fibrous plaster. The 'fibrous' ingredient was canvas or scrim used to strengthen the plaster so that large or long items, such as complete lengths of cornice, could be cast in the workshop and brought to site.

In his comprehensive handbook, *Plastering: plain and decorative* (1897), William Millar was enthusiastic about the advantages of fibrous plaster:

> Its great lightness is a decided point in its favour, as it does not tend to pull down the lath and plaster, but when properly screwed up into the joists, or even the laths, it becomes a support to the three-coat plaster ceiling. An ordinary-sized centre flower can be securely fixed with eight or twelve screws, and without disturbing the lime-plastered ceiling, thus avoiding damp, dust, or dirt, as generally caused when fixing solid plaster centre flowers, which require the ceiling to be cut for keying purposes. A well-made fibrous centre flower, 2 feet in diameter, only weighs about 4lbs. Therefore it would now be possible to send a centre flower by parcels post!

Once the plaster was dry the plasterer had to 'white' (paint with limewash) the ceilings and walls of the cellar, kitchen, service areas and servants' rooms, and prepare the walls of the better rooms for painting. His work was priced at several rates: flat plaster was measured by the superficial (i.e. square) yard, cornices by the superficial foot; enrichments to cornices by the linear foot; and centre flowers and other decorations per piece, according to size and complexity.

A diagram for construction of running mould for a plaster cornice, from William Millar's *Plastering: Plain and Decorative*. The metal plate cut to the desired profile was 'horsed' (supported with timber backing and struts) so that it could be held and would not bend in use. The moulding in the corners would be done by hand.

37

Above: A ceiling rose of about 1840. The moulded frame was run on the ceiling, before the rose was fixed into place. Each of the acanthus leaves was individually cast, then applied to a backing of laths that was screwed into the joists. The beaded enrichments were cast and added separately.

Right: The architectural ceramics industry flourished as indoor plumbing became the norm, and manufacturers' catalogues suggested elaborately tiled settings for the latest models of WC.

Far right: Innovative electric lighting was being fitted by the end of Victoria's reign.

PLUMBING

Due to the absence of indoor plumbing, early Victorian specifications for plumbers' work were more likely to mention roofs and rainwater goods than internal pipework. Plumbers provided sheet roofing, flashings, gutter linings, downpipes and cisterns. They worked with sheet lead produced by pouring molten metal onto a bed of sand and allowing it to cool. The plumber would do this himself if old lead was available for re-use; otherwise he would buy milled lead (cast and rolled metal). Although this cost more, it had a more consistent thickness and quality, without the pinholes and bubbles that could occur in the cast material. The sheets were joined with rolled and lapped joints that allowed the metal to expand and shrink with changing temperatures.

The plumber used a beechwood 'bat' to 'dress' or shape the lead by beating it (this made the metal malleable) over wooden formers. Downpipes were made by dressing a sheet of lead around a wooden dowel and soldering along the seam with molten lead. Sheet lead was also used for lining sinks and cisterns. From about 1850, these items were superseded by cast-iron rainwater goods and fireclay sinks.

Plumbers, painters and glaziers were closely associated because lead was used in all three trades: for roofs and pipework, for the H-section 'cames' in

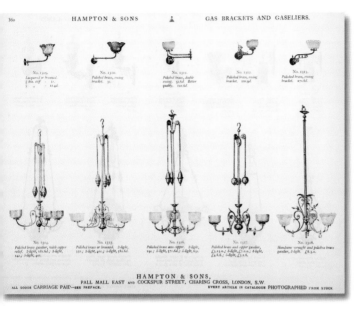

HAMPTON & SONS   GAS BRACKETS AND GASELIERS.

HAMPTON & SONS,
PALL MALL EAST and COCKSPUR STREET, CHARING CROSS, LONDON, S.W
ALL GOODS CARRIAGE PAID—SEE PREFACE.   EVERY ARTICLE IN CATALOGUE PHOTOGRAPHED FROM STOCK

Left: In the last quarter of the nineteenth century, several forms of lighting were in use simultaneously, and retailers' catalogues frequently contain images of oil, gas and electric lights in the same edition. Plumbers found it easy to transfer their attention from creating networks of pipes for water or gas, to installing cables for electricity.

Below: The development of plate glass made it possible to have single-pane sashes from about 1840. The absence of internal glazing bars made the sash less rigid, so the stiles of the upper sash had to be lengthened into 'horns' to make a stronger joint.

leaded lights, and – in the form of white lead – as a paint ingredient. Because they were accustomed to pipework, plumbers also dealt with the gas supply, installed the pulleys and wires that operated the servants' bells, and even installed some early electrical systems.

Of all trades on the Victorian building site, plumbing was the one most affected by the advent of new technology. During the nineteenth century modern services became the norm in new housing: mains water replaced wells and pumps; sewers replaced cesspits; WCs and baths were plumbed-in, and gas was used for cooking, hot water and lighting. Such developments encouraged lead workers to specialise in one or other branch of their trade.

The glazier had to fit glass to the windows as soon as the casements or sashes were installed. The best glass available in the early nineteenth century was crown glass from Newcastle, which arrived on site in 'tables' or discs of about 3 feet in diameter, packed in straw. The glazier used a 'grozing iron' and later a diamond cutter to cut these into usable panes. In 1832, Chance Brothers & Co. of Birmingham patented a new method of making high-quality plate glass. The availability of large sheets of glass of consistent

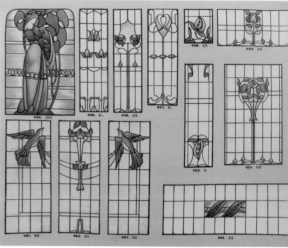

Above:
Ready-made
stained-glass front
door panels were
a colourful feature
of late-Victorian
suburban houses.

Above right:
This selection
of ready-made
designs is from
an early twentieth-
century catalogue
published by Shaw
& Co, a firm
of builders'
merchants

Opposite bottom:
Victorian
decorators were
accustomed to
layering different
finishes to achieve
different effects.
This sample card
demonstrates the
use of varnish to
deepen the colour
of a paint, give it a
glossy surface and
make it more
hardwearing.

quality at an affordable price, and the abolition of the window tax in 1851 meant that large, single-pane sashes became the norm in most houses, multiple glazing bars and leaded lights continuing in use for reasons of taste or fashion rather than necessity.

Plumbers were aware of the danger of lead poisoning: molten lead gave off toxic fumes during the casting process, and the metal could poison through contact with the skin. Painters too had to take care, since white lead powder was a prime ingredient of oil paints. The census for 1891 showed that there were 132,010 persons 'employed in lead processes' and 123,825 of these were painters. Even surface preparation could be hazardous, because using a paraffin torch-lamp and shavehook to remove old oil paint created lead fumes.

PAINTING AND DECORATING

Because his work came at the end of the construction process, the painter and decorator was usually under pressure to complete his work quickly so that the house could be sold. Developers could not wait for the structure to dry out before starting to decorate. Consequently, the first decoration in a new house would be the 'builder's finish' of distemper, a cheap, permeable, water-based paint that provided a respectable appearance and allowed the structure to 'breathe'. In any subsequent redecorating, the distemper was washed off before new paint was applied. This removed soot and dirt and ensured that decorative plasterwork retained its crisp outlines.

Paints were mixed by hand on site, using traditional recipes. Oil paint was made by mixing an opaque 'body colour' of white lead with linseed oil and a drier such as turpentine. The proportions of oil and drier determined how glossy the painted surface would be. The body colour in water-based paints was provided by whiting (powdered chalk). Pigments made from earths, minerals and plant or animal extracts were added to obtain the desired colour; these were ground in portable mills, or by hand using a glass 'muller' on a stone slab.

In Whittock's illustration of painters at work, one man uses a long-haired paintbrush or 'flogger', perhaps for a dragged paint effect, while another uses a fine brush to highlight a moulding with a contrasting colour. In the foreground, an apprentice grinds pigments with a glass muller on a grindstone.

Paint recipes had to compensate for the fact that some colours were unstable: linseed oil, for example, would darken and yellow over time, so a small amount of blue pigment would be added to white paint as an optical brightener to keep it looking fresh.

It was not until the end of the nineteenth century that ready-mixed paint became widely available. Until then, each batch of paint was mixed as needed. It was almost impossible to match the colour of two batches, so the decorator had to judge exactly how much would be required to finish the job in hand. In *The Diary of a Nobody*, this gives a tradesman the perfect excuse to exaggerate a quote:

> ... he could not match the colour on the stairs, as it contained Indian carmine. He said he spent half-a-day calling at warehouses to see if he could get it. He suggested he should entirely repaint the stairs. It would cost very little more; if he tried to match it, he could only make a bad job of it. It would be more satisfactory to him and to us to have the work done properly ... I consented, but felt I had been talked over.

The decorator had to master different application techniques for hand-made paints, which were temperamental and inconsistent. Distemper, for example, would dry quickly and leave a tidemark along the leading edge unless applied with rapid, confident brushstrokes. The choice of finish was guided by the relative durability of different surfaces, which made them more or less suitable for certain locations: hall dados, for example, were painted with dark colours and varnished to protect

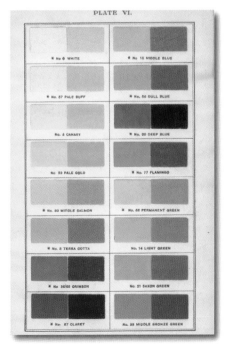

PLATE VI.

* No 6 WHITE | * No 18 MIDDLE BLUE
* No. 87 PALE BUFF | * No. 50 DULL BLUE
No. 5 CANARY | * No. 20 DEEP BLUE
No. 29 PALE GOLD | * No. 77 FLAMINGO
* No. 90 MIDDLE SALMON | * No. 68 PERMANENT GREEN
* No. 8 TERRA COTTA | No. 14 LIGHT GREEN
* No 56/66 CRIMSON | No. 21 SAXON GREEN
* No. 87 CLARET | No. 39 MIDDLE BRONZE GREEN

The *Decorative Painter and Glazier's Guide* by Nathaniel Whittock (1828) provided samples of wood graining and other imitative finishes, with detailed instructions on how to achieve them.

hem from wear. Softwood surfaces, inside and out,
were always painted, with 'two or three coats of
good oil colour'. Oak, on the other hand, was
varnished, to show off its grain.

A decorator had to be able to apply imitative
finishes including marbling, gilding and wood
graining. The latter was used to give softwood the
appearance of more expensive timber such as oak
or mahogany, and for surfaces that would receive
heavy usage: on a kitchen door, for instance, the
'broken' appearance of graining helped to disguise
chips and scratches.

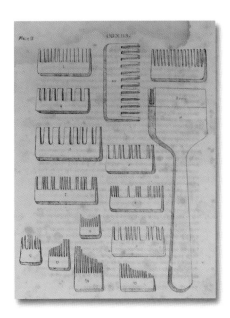

Nathaniel Whittock's *Decorative Painter and
Glazier's Guide* (1828) described how to imitate
Parian, Carrara, Florentine, Sienna, brocatello
and serpentine marbles, and porphyry, but the
decorator's art consisted of knowing where to use
such finishes. Tressell wrote scathingly of a labourer
who 'had "picked up" a slight knowledge of the
trade, and having armed himself with a putty-knife and put on a white jacket,
regarded himself as a fully qualified painter'. In contrast, his hero, Owen,
has the ideal combination of technical knowledge, skill and taste to design
high-class decorative schemes:

A handle with a set
of interchangeable
combs for achieving
a variety of paint
effects.

> The walls divided into panels and arches containing painted designs and
> lattice-work. The panels of the door decorated in a similar manner. The
> mouldings of the door and window frames picked out with colours and
> gold so as to be in character with the other work; the cove of the cornice, a
> dull yellow with a bold ornament in colour – gold was not advisable in the
> hollow because of the unequal distribution of the light, but some of the
> smaller mouldings of the cornice should be in gold .... Process by process
> he traced the work, and saw it advancing stage by stage until, finally, the
> large apartment was transformed and glorified.

There was no shortage of advice on colour schemes and finishes. In *Studies in
Design* (1874), the designer Christopher Dresser declared:

> A white skirting should never exist. I often make the skirting black, but in this
> case I generally polish or varnish the greater portion of it, yet leave parts 'dead',
> thus getting a contrast between a bright and a dead surface. I sometimes run
> a few lines of colour upon its mouldings, but I never in any way ornament it.
> It should be retiring and bold .... If not black, it may often advantageously be

brown, rich maroon, dull blue, or bronze-green. Even in light rooms it should be considerably darker than the walls.

Decoration underlined the status and use of each room. 'Masculine' dining rooms or studies were decorated in darker colours than 'feminine' drawing rooms. Elaborate paint effects and colour combinations were used to 'pick in' mouldings in reception rooms where they could be appreciated by visitors, but not in kitchens or nurseries used only by servants and children.

Exterior stucco and render were painted to reinforce the illusion of a stone façade. A solution of copperas in limewater would give the appearance of Bath stone, and splattered pigments created the impression of lichen spreading across ancient masonry. Sand mixed into the paint produced a textured finish that enhanced the stone effect. Loudon considered, logically, that 'the kinds of colours most suitable for exterior walls should generally be such as belong to the stones or bricks of the county in which the dwelling stands.'

The showroom of the high-class decorators Wannop & Son of Liverpool, photographed in 1890. The walls are lined with samples of imitative finishes and decorative painting.

WORKING LIFE

HOURS AND TRAVEL TO WORK

A WELL-ESTABLISHED FIRM with a permanent workforce might allow some travelling time in the working day: Walter Rose's grandfather paid his men for the time it took them to walk up to six miles to site, but expected them to walk home – a couple of hours at the end of a tiring day – in their own time. For most workmen, the only way to get to work was on foot, which meant leaving home very early. The invention of the safety bicycle in the late 1880s transformed travel to work, especially in country districts: by speeding up journey times, it greatly increased the radius within which a man could seek work.

Public transport made travel easier for builders in cities and inner suburbs, although its use, like all other aspects of Victorian life, was dictated by stringent social codes as well as cost. An Act of Parliament in 1864 obliged the Great Eastern Railway to provide an early-morning, cheap train service. Although slow to comply, eventually the GER were running more 'workmen's trains' than the Act required. In 1882 they complained to a Parliamentary Commission that it had become impossible to stop running the trains although the service lost money: workmen tracked dirt into the carriages, which could not then be used for other passengers, and their behaviour (particularly spitting on the platforms) deterred middle-class travellers. Unmoved, Parliament the following year passed the Cheap Trains Act, which required train companies to provide workmen's trains after six o'clock in the evening and before eight in the morning, at fares of less than 1d per mile – but it was not enforced and compliance was patchy.

Punch, June 1868, comments on the unwillingness of railway companies to provide cheap trains for working men unless forced to by legislation. The peer, representing the House of Lords, is interceding on behalf of the carpenter to ensure that the latter is not overcharged for his ticket.

No workman would take an omnibus: it was expensive, and the service started too late in the morning for men who had to be on site by eight o'clock The *Cornhill Magazine* in 1890 stated that 'the working man is rarely seen on the upholstered cushions [of the omnibus] … he feels himself uncomfortable and *de trop*. The tramcar is *his* familiar vehicle and he can ensconce himself there in his mortar-splashed clothes without restraint.' Tram companies, like the railways, were obliged to offer workmen's fares and by the early 1900s in boroughs such as East Ham where they were under municipal control, they provided an extensive network at an affordable price.

However he travelled, the Victorian workman started work early, at between six and eight every morning, including Saturdays. The working day ended at dusk, so construction work was seasonal, with fifty-hour weeks in summer and little or no work in winter. The weather was the other main influence on the working calendar. Frost made lime-based mortar unworkable, so bricklayers were forced to down trowels from October to the following spring. It was dangerous to excavate basements during rain, as a pit could quickly fill up with water and become a treacherous quagmire Mayhew in 1851 commented on paviours, pipe-layers, bricklayers, house painters and slaters, who could not work on wet days, watching for change in the weather 'with a terrible interest'.

WAGES AND CONDITIONS

City builders were better paid than their country cousins, and London builders earned most of all: 'skilled workmen sent to the country from London receive their usual London wages, and in addition thereto all travelling expenses and the whole cost of their lodging in the country,' noted Kerr. He thought that building works were generally 5–10 per cent cheaper in the country, although the difference could be as much as 25 per cent. On the other hand, country jobs might be further away from the builder's headquarters, with the attendant loss of time and the cost of transporting building materials.

It is difficult to relate wages to standards of living, as there are many variables besides equivalent values in today's money. Rural wages were low but could be supplemented with free firewood or garden produce, so a country builder might live as comfortably as his better-paid London counterpart Perhaps the worst-off were builders in provincial towns. In Lincoln in 1857 labourers were paid 9d a day. 'Others were working for 12s. a week, and after paying rent there was perhaps 2s. a head for food and clothing; they work on bread with sometimes a morsel of bacon and cheese.' This was at a time when according to Thomas Miller of Gainsborough, a family of six needed 7s 6d a week for the barest necessities: 'rent, clothes, bread, coal, candle and soap small beer and potatoes, flour, lard and milk'. Another 7s would be required

Punch took a robustly anti-union line in the 1859 London builders' strike. This cartoon by John Leech, published on 5 November 1859, suggests that the strikers were being manipulated by union organisers who themselves had nothing to lose: a well-fed 'committee man and general talker' urges a striker to 'hold out', even though he and his family are on the brink of starvation.

for 'common necessities extra – meat, tea and coffee'. Wages could be knocked back in hard times: in the lean year of 1864 the Lincoln stonemasons agreed to accept a weekly wage of 25s – more or less what they had been receiving ten years earlier.

A journeyman carpenter in the country received 17s or 18s for a sixty-hour week around 1880; this rose to 21s by the end of the century. In 1894, according to Dobson, London journeymen in most trades were paid around 5s a day. The wages of bricklayers, masons and plumbers were slightly higher, perhaps 5s 6d per day. Masons on piecework, or any work requiring particular skill, earned much more. The same applied to plasterers: 'The wages of a journeyman plasterer are from 4s to 5s a day; those engaged in modelling and ornamental work will earn much more; a labourer receives from 2s 6d to 3s a day, and a plasterer's boy about 1s.' Labourers – who were between 20 and 30 per cent of the construction workforce in the last quarter of the nineteenth century – earned roughly half the wages paid to their masters.

Robert Tressell described a general labourer working for 4d an hour (which tallies with Dobson's 3s per day), and time-served craftsmen anxiously trying to negotiate fair wages in competition with men who were ready to work for 2d an hour less than the standard rate. His rage was justified: Booth's classifications of the London poor in 1898 included most categories of builder, from labourers and poorer artisans with intermittent earnings of '18s to 21s per week for a moderate family' to the best-paid artisans and foremen, who earned more than 30s per week. Despite 'good character and much

the handle of the Hod mon at right angle

George Scharf's sketch of people heading to work in the early morning includes carpenters, joiners, masons and pavers. The cast of characters includes a carpenter with a sawhorse over his shoulder, a bricklayer with a bundle in his hod, a labourer who hooks the handle of his shovel over the blade of his pickaxe, and a mason with square, plumb rule and mallet wedged under his arms.

intelligence', none of the skilled men earned enough to enter the lower middle class of shopkeepers and clerks.

It was difficult for builders to organise their labour. The industry had a fragmented workforce working in ever-changing locations. Each trade jealously controlled its status, apprenticeships and standards, and was unwilling to join forces with others. Complex methods of payment – piecework, day rate, hourly rate, fixed price – made negotiations difficult, and the widespread use of sub-contractors and self-employed or casual workers prevented collective bargaining.

Early attempts to form building workers' unions coincided with the emergence of large contractors such as Cubitt's and George Trollope & Sons in the 1820s and '30s. These firms brought together large numbers of workers in single organisations, and also provided a focus for the discontents of small masters and journeymen, who could not compete with the larger firms' prices. The Operative Builders' Union was an association of trades societies formed in 1831 to prevent 'inferior men' from undercutting skilled workers' wages, and to resist the exploitative sub-contracts. Its collapse in 1834 destroyed the hope of forming an industry-wide union; instead, labour became organised on trade lines, which left it weak and fragmented. Within each trade, union membership was sparse: barely 25 per cent of eligible workers joined the Operative Stone Masons Society in the 1870s, and the Amalgamated Society of Carpenters and Joiners did not recruit more than 10 per cent of the woodworkers in the country until the 1890s.

The most sustained attempt to obtain better conditions in the building industry was a campaign in the 1850s for a shorter working week. In 1857 the Manchester Committee of Trades demanded a Saturday leaving time of 1 p.m. (previous demands for a 4 p.m. knocking-off time having partly succeeded), and in 1858 an *ad hoc* committee of London-based tradesmen, led by George Potter, demanded a nine-hour working day. Their campaign came to a head in July 1959, when Trollope's dismissed a group of masons who had petitioned for shorter hours, and all their masons went on strike in protest. Within a fortnight, 225 London firms, each employing more than fifty men, shut their gates, leaving some 24,000 men without work. The lockout lasted for eight weeks before both sides came to terms, with no firm resolution of the original question.

CLOTHES AND EQUIPMENT

Tressell described builders allocating a portion of their weekly wage to purchasing clothes on credit:

> Some of them had to pay a shilling a week to a tallyman or credit clothier.
> These were the ones who indulged in shoddy new suits – at long intervals.
> Others bought ... their clothes at second-hand shops, 'paying off' about a
> shilling or so a week and not receiving the things till they were paid for.

The working outfit consisted of trousers, jacket and waistcoat. Shirts were worn collarless and unbuttoned, with a cotton handkerchief round the neck in summer to mop away sweat, and a woollen scarf in winter. In hot weather the jacket might be removed and the waistcoat unbuttoned, but under no circumstances would a workman take off his shirt.

Corduroy trousers were warm, comfortable and hard-wearing, with enough 'give' in the fabric to allow the wearer to move freely. A street-seller of men's second-hand clothes told Mayhew he could always sell trousers, especially 'good strong cords [which] goes off very well at 1s. and 1s 6d., or higher. Irish bricklayers buys them, and paviours, and such like.'

For additional freedom of movement, trousers were hitched up under the knee with a leather strap or piece of twine. Walter Rose noted a further adaptation to the carpenter's cords: a special long pocket in the right leg to accommodate a folding two-foot rule. 'This pocket the town tailors persisted in placing too low, with the result that the rule acted as a splint, an impediment to the bending of the knee … so the trouser trade from our shop flowed to the village tailor who had brain enough to understand the need.'

White jackets were worn by painters and decorators to protect their clothing from paint spatters, and aprons were favoured by many tradesmen especially painters and carpenters.

For most of the Victorian period British cities grew by outward expansion so builders were nearly always working on greenfield sites with unmade roads, in mud, and a comfortable pair of stout leather boots was essential. Contemporary images depict navvies wearing a form of leather Wellington boots with wide tops turned over. Most builders favoured lace-up boots, with hobnails punched into the soles for grip.

Some form of headgear was essential; quite simply (in any context, not only building sites), a man was not decently dressed without a hat. In the late nineteenth century most workmen wore flat caps in tweed, while the bowler hat was favoured by foremen and senior tradesmen. During the working day, many builders would wear a box-shaped 'printer's hat' of folded newspaper, which could be thrown away and replaced as needed. The printer's hat was favoured by painters and decorators, for obvious reasons, but was also associated with carpenters, perhaps because of Tenniel's illustration of the Walrus and the Carpenter in *Through the Looking-glass*.

The other essential element of the builder's outfit was his tools. Master craftsmen and journeymen had their own tools, which they carried with them from job to job, and provided tools for their apprentices and labourers. Carpenters kept their tools in rush baskets with leather-bound handles which they slung over their shoulders. Plumbers used drawstring bags that opened out flat for the tools to be set out at the start of the job. Large sets of tools were kept in stout, lockable deal chests.

Tools were the personal property of each craftsman, and a source of pride and concern throughout his working life. For Walter Rose, part of the satisfaction of making sash windows derived from the specialist tools required for the job:

> Every workman aspired to possess his complete set of sash ovolo moulding plans; his sash fillister for taking out the rebates to receive the glass; his brass-ended mitres for fitting the ends of the sash bars; his double-tooth gauge and mortise chisels … many would keep specially prepared steel scribing blades with points ranged at the exact distance apart for setting out the sashes.

Apprentices built up their own sets of tools by making them, inheriting them from retired craftsmen or buying second-hand items. A complete set assembled over several years, represented a considerable investment — twenty-four pages of Peter Nicholson's *New Practical Builder* are devoted to carpenters' tools – so the owner would chisel his name or initials into the handles. Tools were rarely shared and borrowing was frowned upon; in any case, through long use a tool would become worn to its owner's hand, so that another man would find it awkward to use.

Care was taken to keep blades clean and sharp. A carpenter would squint along the line of his saw to check

The art of setting and sharpening a saw was not easy to acquire. Craftsmen took pride in keeping their equipment in good order, and would not entrust their favourite tools to apprentices.

for straightness, then use a file to sharpen and align each tooth. Nicholson, a cabinetmaker and joiner, explained the process of sharpening and 'setting' a saw in detail, and criticised journeymen who wasted time and money taking their tools to professional sharpeners.

Blades were sharpened with oilstones. These were sold by weight, a woodworking manual published in 1875 stating that 'Turkey-stone' was the dearest, 'and also by far the best.' In 1889 the Washita, a natural stone from Wichita, was introduced to England, and quickly found to be superior to the native Charnley Forest stones that had dominated the market until then. Around 1890 the artificial stone Carborundum made its first appearance. Years of use would wear a stone to its owner's hand so that no other man could use it comfortably.

FOOD AND DRINK

In 1900 most building sites were still being cleared and walls raised by muscle power alone, and most of the calories the Victorian builder needed to fuel strenuous physical activity through a long working day came from the carbohydrates in bread; the commonest on-site lunch was bread and cheese.

According to Tressell, the dinner hour was announced by a blast on the foreman's whistle, whereupon:

> … all hands assembled in the kitchen, where Bert the apprentice had already
> prepared the tea [in a] large galvanized iron pail …. By the side of the pail

were a number of old jam-jars, mugs, dilapidated tea-cups and one or two empty condensed milk tins. Each man on the 'job' paid Bert threepence a week for the tea and sugar – they did not have milk – and although they had tea at breakfast-time as well as at dinner, the lad was generally considered to be making a fortune.

Victorian builders, like their modern counterparts, were enthusiastic patrons of take-away food and drink stalls. Among the dishes that are unfashionable now but eaten with relish by the Victorian workman were sheep's trotters, boiled puddings and plum duff, as well as the cockney classics: pea-soup, stewed eels, whelks, winkles and bloaters. A popular hot drink sold on the streets in the early Victorian period was saloop, a kind of sweet, milky tea made with powdered sassafras root and sugar. By 1850, this had been superseded by coffee. Mayhew recorded that the holders of the best coffee-stall pitches in London did a 24-hour trade, some opening at four or five in the morning, 'for the accommodation of the working men'. A penny bought a mug of coffee and the chance to warm oneself for a few minutes at the heat of the urn before heading to work.

The other great place of relaxation for the Victorian workman was the pub, which reached a great pitch of specialisation in the nineteenth century with separate 'public' bars where men could go for a drink in their work clothes without feeling inappropriately dressed.

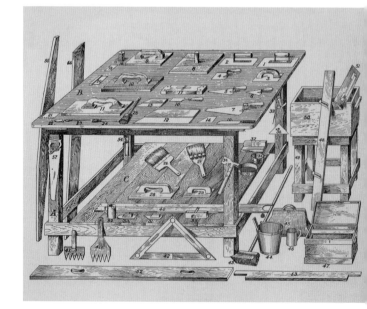

It would take a craftsman many years to build up his stock of tools. William Millar, with characteristic thoroughness, depicted every last item that a master plasterer might need in the course of a working life.

CONCLUSION

THE AMALGAMATION of separate building trades into firms of 'general builders' was an established trend by 1900, and one which gathered momentum throughout the twentieth century. Increasing mechanisation and the introduction of power tools have enabled multi-skilled workers to take over jobs that were once the preserve of highly trained specialists; prefabrication and new technology have recast the building site as an assembly line where shrink-wrapped components are slotted together like three-dimensional jigsaw puzzles; immeasurably better standards of health, safety and on-site welfare have transformed the sprawling, muddy chaos of Victorian developments into hoarding-enclosed worlds with security gates leading to Portakabin canteens and locker rooms. Construction companies

A remodelled entrance hall, from *Interior Decorating* by Duncan Miller, first published in 1933 and re-issued after the Second World War. The mid-twentieth-century fashion for clean lines and flat surfaces encouraged owners of Victorian houses to to conceal original detailed decoration. Nowadays such features – and the craftsmanship that went into making them – are once again highly prized.

on a scale undreamt of by Cubitt and his contemporaries now dominate the building industry, and small concerns have been squeezed out to the margins.

And yet, there is much that the Victorian builder would find familiar, particularly at the jobbing or small development end of the market. Self-employed builders continue to value the autonomy and independence of working for themselves, and the more ambitious still start their own firms, prepared to be, as Walter Rose put it in 1913, 'manager, general foreman, workman, draughtsman, estimator, book-keeper, and correspondent – all these offices must be represented in himself if the small concern is to be kept going.'

Traditional craft skills such as carpentry, stone carving, rubbed brickwork, gilding and graining are still practised, even if restricted to conservation and luxury projects.

Victorian houses still make desirable homes, and there is work for builders with the skills to repair and restore original features such as timber sash windows and cast-iron fireplaces, which were ill-advisedly discarded during the modernisation frenzy of the post-war period.

Above all, there is still a need for decent, affordable family accommodation in the modern equivalent of the Victorian terraced house, semi or mansion flat. Whatever form the next generation of modest, middle-market housing takes, it is certain that its builders will not surpass the persistence, ingenuity and willing spirit of the men who built the Victorian suburbs.

This page from a hardware catalogue shows that, despite increasing standardisation, the Victorian builder still had access to a plethora of fittings, even when it came to the simple handles used to raise a sash window.

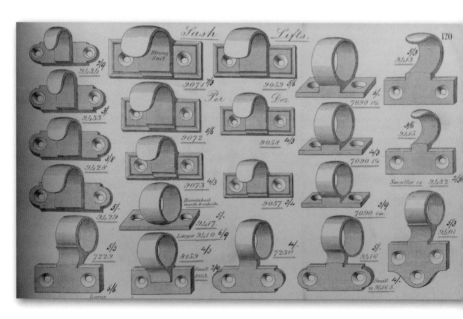

FURTHER READING

Ayres, James. *Building the Georgian City*. Yale University Press, 1998.

Barrett, Helena, and Phillips, John. *Suburban Style: The British Home 1840–1960*. Macdonald Orbis, 1987.

Burnett, John. *A Social History of Housing 1815 – 1970*. Methuen, 1980.

Cannadine, David, and David Reeder (eds.). *Exploring the Urban Past: Essays in Urban History by H.J. Dyos*. Cambridge University Press, 1982.

Cruickshank, Dan, and Neil Burton. *Life in the Georgian City*. Viking, 1990.

Dobson, Edward. *The Art of Building* (14th edn.). Crosby Lockwood & Son, 1894.

Girouard, Mark. *Sweetness and Light: The Queen Anne Movement 1860–1900*. Yale University Press, 1984.

Grossmith, George and Weedon. *Diary of a Nobody* (1892). Digital edition: http://www.gutenberg.org/ebooks/1026.

Gwilt, Joseph. *An Encyclopaedia of Architecture, Historic, Theoretical, and Practical*. Longman, 1842.

Hobhouse, Hermione. *Thomas Cubitt, Master Builder*. Macmillan, 1971.

Kerr, Robert. *The Gentleman's House* (3rd edn., 1871). Johnson Reprint Corporation, 1972.

Loudon, J.C. *The Encyclopaedia of Cottage, Farm, and Villa Architecture* (1846). Donhead, 2000.

Mayhew, Henry. *London Labour and the London Poor*, Vol. 2 (1851). Digital edition: http://hdl.handle.net/10427/14951.

Millar, William. *Plastering: Plain and Decorative* (1897). Donhead, 1998.

Muthesius, Hermann. *The English House* (1904). BSP Professional Books, 1987.

Muthesius, Stefan. *The English Terraced House*. Yale University Press, 1982.

Olsen, Donald J. *The Growth of Victorian London*. B.T. Batsford, 1976.

Rose, Walter. *The Village Carpenter* (1937). Stobart Davies, 2009.

Summerson, John. *The London Building World of the Eighteen-Sixties*. Thames and Hudson, 1973.

Robert Tressell, *The Ragged-Trousered Philanthropists* (1911). Penguin Classics, 2004.

Young & Marten, *The Victorian House Catalogue* (1897). Sidgwick & Jackson/The Victorian Society, 1990.

INDEX

Page numbers in *italic* refer to illustrations.

Amalgamated Society of Carpenters and Joiners 49
Arch, rubbed brickwork *28*
Architects 18–19
Art of Building, The 6, 47
'Back-to-back' houses 11
Balusters *33*
BBC television *53*
Booth, Charles 5, 47
Bricklayers/Bricklaying 8, 26–7, *26, 27,* 29–30, 34
Brickwork, polychromatic 19, *19, 28,* 29
Bristol: builders in 15, *15;* stonework 8, *8*
Bucknell, Barry *53*
Builder, The 6
Builder's Practical Director 18
Builders' merchants' catalogues 7
Building Acts 8, 17–18
Building News 6, 15, 20
Building sites, work on 21, 24–7, 29–41, 43–4; bricklaying 26–7, *26, 27,* 29–30, 34; carpentry 32, 34; decorating 40–1, *40,* 43–4, *44;* excavation 24–5; foremen 21, 24; glazing 39–40, *39, 40;* joinery 32, *32,* 34; masonry 30–2, *30;* painting 39, 40–1, *41, 42,* 43–4, *43, 44;* plastering 35–8, *36, 37, 38;* plumbing 38–9, *38,* 40; roofing 34–5, *35;* scaffolding 25–6, *25;* timber selection 32–4, *33;* training 21
Carpenter's family home *5*
Carpentry 32, 34
Ceramics, architectural *38*
Chance Brothers & Co. 40
Cheap Trains Act 1883 45
Chimneypieces, enamelled slate *31*

Cornhill Magazine 46
Cornices 6, 36, 37–8, *37*
'Cottages, working-class' *6*
Cubitt, Thomas 12–13, *12,* 48
Decorating 40–1, *40,* 43–4, *44*
Decorative mouldings 6, 36–8, *37, 38;* panels, Japanese-style carved or moulded *29,* 30
Decorative paint finishes *42,* 43–4, *43, 44*
Decorative Painter and Glazier's Guide 42, 43
Designs 17–20; styles 19, *19,* 20, *21,* 29–30; suburban houses 20
Diary of a Nobody 13, 14–15, 41
Dobson, Edward 32, 47
Door, front, stained glass panels *40*
Dresser, Christopher 43–4
East Malling, Kent *28*
Electric lighting *38, 39*
Elmes, James 13
Encyclopedia of Cottage, Farm and Villa Architecture 6, *6,* 8, 44
Engels, Friedrich 11
Excavations 24–5
Fittings *54*
Foremen 21, 24
'Fourth-rate' houses *18*
Gentleman's House, The 19, 21, 24, 46
Glazing 39–40, *39, 40*
Great Eastern Railway 45
Grossmith, George *13,* 14–15, 41
Grosvenor Estate 12, 13
Hardy, Thomas 31
Houseowner's Estimator 18
Improved Industrial Dwellings Company 18, *19*
Instruction books *8*
Joinery 32, *32,* 34
Jude the Obscure 31
Kerr, Robert 19, 21, 24, 46
Lead, working with 38–9, 40

Leasehold system 11–12
Lighting *38, 39*
Lincoln, wages in 46–7
London: Bedford Park *17;* Belgrave Square 12–13, *12;* Belgravia 12–13; Bethnal Green *18;* Bethnal Green, Boundary Estate 18, *35;* builders in 15; Pimlico 13; suburbs 11
London Building Act 1774 17
London County Council 18, 35
London Going Out of Town… (cartoon) *4*
Loudon, J. C. 6, *6,* 8, 44
Manchester Committee of Trades 49
Masonry 30–2, *30*
Mass production 7, 8, 20
Mayhew, Henry 5, 46, 49, 52
Middle-class housing 20, *20*
Millar, William 37, *37, 52*
Miller, Thomas 46–7
Modernisation, post-war 53, 54
New Practical Builder 51
Nicholson, Peter 51
Operative Builders' Union 48–9
Operative Stone Masons Society 49
Oxford, North *19*
Oxford, Osney *28*
Oxford University Museum *30*
Painting 39, 40–1, *41, 42,* 43–4, *43, 44*
Paints 39, 40–1, *40,* 43
Papworth, J. W. 11
Peabody Trust 18
Plastering 35–8, *36, 37, 38*
Plastering: plain and decorative 37, *37,* 52
Plumbing 38–9, *38,* 40
Potter, George 49
Pricing 21, 24
Pugin, A. W. N. 18
Punch magazine 5, *5, 13,* 45, *47*

'Queen Anne' houses *17,* 19, 29–30
Ragged-trousered Philanthropists, The 5, 24, 43, 47, 49, 51–2
Railway travel 45, *45*
Reading, bricks in 8, *8*
Roofing 34–5, *35*
Rose, Walter 8, 21, 34, 49–50, 54; brother 21; grandfather 33, 45
Ruskin, John 18
Sawyers 33–4
Scaffolding 25–6, *25*
'Scamping' 5, *13,* 24
Sessions (Jesse) & Co 31
Shaw, Richard Norman 6, 3
Stonework 30–2, *30*
Studies in Design 43–4
Suburban development 4, 8, 11–15, 20
Summerson, Sir John 4, 13
Terraced housing 11, *14, 18;* first class *12*
Timber and timber merchants 32–4, *33*
Tools 50–1, *52;* bricklayer 29; masonry *30;* sharpening 51, *51*
Trade unions 47, 48–9
Tressell, Robert 5, 24, 43, 47, 49, 51–2
Trollope (George) & Sons 48, 49
Wannop & Son *44*
Watts of Catford 15
Whittock, Nathaniel 33–4 *41, 42,* 43
Window, joinery elements 32
Woodwork *33,* 34
'Working-class' housing 6, 11, *14, 18, 19*
Working life 45–52; clothes *48,* 49–51; conditions *47,* 48–9; equipment 50–1; food and drink 51–2; hours of work 45, 46; travel to work 45–6, *45;* wages 46–8